Welcome to the w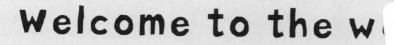 COPYING

Use pens to draw over the dotted lines and copy the pictures in this book.

This is Arty Mouse.
Copy **1** ear and **2** whiskers.

Summer flowers

Arty Mouse loves flowers. Copy the petal shapes to finish the picture.

Add some color to your flower.

Finish these summer flowers, too.

springtime nest

Copy the egg shapes to fill mommy bird's nest.

Rainbow bird

How many eggs will you draw?

Bedtime!

Dot wants a sleeping bag
to match Stripy's.
Can you help to finish it?

Shapes fun

Geo loves shapes! Copy the shapes
to finish each row.

Geo

Don't forget
to color in
your shapes!

Help Stripy to copy the shapes in the little house to make a big house.

Scribble's fish

Scribble is looking at the fish's shapes.

Scribble

Copy my fish into the empty bowls.
Then color each one.

Happy robot

Copy the shapes to finish
the picture of Geo.

color in
the rest
of me!

wonderful waves

Arty Mouse is having
fun in his boat.

Fill the sea with more wavy lines.

Scary waves!

Splat is sailing on
the stormy sea.

splat

Add more big waves, just like these!

Snail shells

Give every snail a spiral shell,
just like Spiro's.

Spiro

Lovely lollipops

Copy these lovely lollipop patterns
to finish Dot's treats.

Big bugs

Give the bugs black spots. Color around the spots with red.

Give me **5** spots!

Give me **6** spots!

Dot's flowers

Dot can see some pretty flowers.
Fill her empty pot with
flowers to match.

A flock of birds

Copy the rainbow bird's shape
to make a flock of birds.

Turn the shapes into
more rainbow birds!

Windy day

A windy day is perfect for flying kites.

Give everyone a kite the same shape as Arty's.

Decorate the kites any way you like.

Add more clouds to this windy scene!

Snowy day

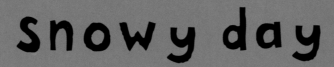

The Arty friends are having fun in the snow.

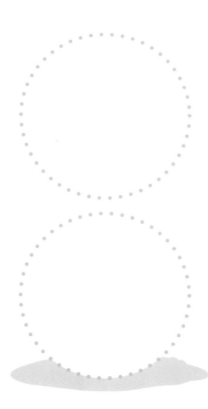

Copy more trees in the distance!

Sssnakes!

Copy the pattern to make all the snakes the same.

Falling leaves
The birds are playing in the falling leaves.

Give every leaf a curly line.

Finish the friends

Copy Arty Mouse's finished half
to complete his picture.

Finish the picture of Dot, too.

Ice cream treats

Help Arty Mouse and Stripy
to choose ice creams.

In the barn

Copy the cat's shape to make her **2** furry friends.

Meow!

1

2

Copy the hen's shape to make her **2** feathery friends.

cluck! cluck!

1

2

Farmyard fun

Look closely at the blue cow.
Copy all the details to complete
the cow below.

Mooo!

Finish the pink pig, too.

Arty Street

Draw everyone a house with shapes like Arty's. Make each house different colors.

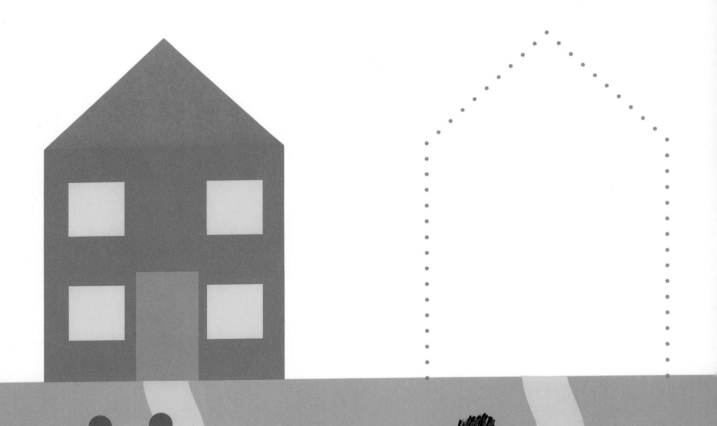

Geo's candies

Can you help Geo to put candies in the empty jars?

Copy the candies from the top jars into the matching jars below.

Look at the jars on the top shelf. Can you copy the candies into the matching jars below?

This is tricky! The jars on the bottom shelf are muddled up!

Fluttering butterfly

Copy the pattern to finish the butterfly, so it can flutter away!

Geo's sandcastle

Geo loves making sandcastles.
Can you make one to match his?

Scribble's mirror

Use your pens or crayons to copy Scribble's reflection in the mirror.

Painting Splat

Help Arty Mouse to
paint Splat's portrait.

Birthday gifts

It's Stripy's birthday! Copy his pile of gifts in the empty space.

I wonder what this could be.

Can you copy more party flags?

Can you make each flag a different color?

Yummy picnic

what would each Arty friend like to eat?

You decide and copy it onto their plate.

Copy and count

Help Geo to fill his boxes with shapes.

2 ⬤

3 ✚

8 ◻

7 ▭

6 ♥

Look at the shape on the label, then copy the right number into each box.

Toy store

Copy each toy to fill the shelves.

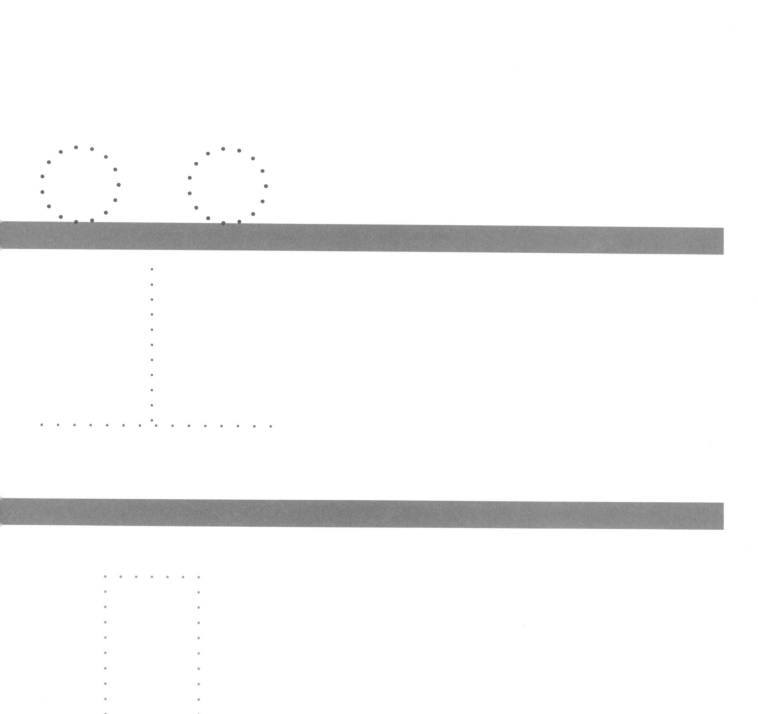

Nighttime sky

Copy more star shapes into the
sky and color them in. Then
color the sky black.